Hooked on
SEAFOOD

by Nana Whalen

The
AMERICAN
★ COOKING ★
GUILD™

Boynton Beach, Florida

Dedication
To John, my resident gourmet, who is always home for dinner no matter what. And to Tim, Ma
and Angela, who are my whole reason for cooking. Together we gather around the kitchen table,
life passes by.

Acknowledgments
—Cover Design and Layout by Pearl & Associates, Inc.
—Cover photo by Burwell and Burwell

More...Quick Recipes for Creative Cooking!
The American Cooking Guild's *Collector's Series* includes over 30 popular cooking topics sucl
Barbeque, Breakfast & Brunches, Chicken, Cookies, Hors d' Oeuvres, Seafood, Tea, Coffee, Pa
Pizza, Salads Italian and many more. Each book contains more than 50 selected recipes. For a
alog of these and many other full sized cookbooks, send $1 to the address below and a coupon
be included for $1 off your first order.

Cookbooks Make Great Premiums!
The American Cooking Guild has been the premier publisher of private label and custom cookbo
since 1981. Retailers, manufacturers, and food companies have all chosen The American Cool
Guild to publish their premium and promotional cookbooks. For further information on our spe
markets programs please contact the address.

The American Cooking Guild
3600-K South Congress Avenue
Boynton Beach, FL 33426

Table of Contents

Chapter I — Hors d'Oeuvres

Chapter II — Sauces & Stuffings

Chapter III — Fish

Chapter IV — Crabs

Chapter V — Oysters

Chapter VI — Shrimp

Chapter VII — Scallops, Clams & Other Delicacies

Foreword

For me, this book is a dream come true. So many hundreds of my readers have asked me to print a collection of recipes from my "Creative Cookery" column which has appeared every Sunday in the Arundel Sun section of the Baltimore Sunpapers for the last 3½ years. Now some of the best recipes are together in one book.

So, this book is dedicated to the "Cooks of the Week" who so willingly shared their most treasured family recipes. Each and every recipe is a winner that has withstood the test of time; many have been passed from generation to generation. I shall always remember each person who shared his/her time and recipes with me. Each cook has enriched my life in so many ways. I have found that all people who love to cook share a common bond of love of the home and service to others.

Whether seafood is a whole new world to you, or you have been experiencing the fruits of the sea all your life, I know you will find some exciting recipes to add to your repertoire. You need never want for a great seafood recipe again.

Happy Cooking,

Nana Whalen

Nana Whalen

Four Steps to Perfect Seafood

1. Buy a Fresh Fish

☐ When buying a fresh, whole fish, these are the things to look for:

flesh — elastic, yet firm; never dull
eyes — bright, clear
gills — red
inside — bright pink or red
odor — mild; avoid fish that has a strong odor

☐ With shellfish, such as clams, oysters, etc., don't buy any that have opened up while raw.

☐ Try to know the source of supply of your seafood. Does the fish come from areas certified by the government to be clean? Has the item been previously frozen? (This may be true with certain out-of-season shellfish, in which case you may not want to refreeze the item.)

2. Buy the Right Amount

Type of Fish	Amount to Buy per Serving
Crab meat	¼ to ⅓ pound
Clams, in the shell — appetizer	6 to 8 clams
Clams, in the shell — entree	15 to 20 clams
Fish, dressed or pan dressed	½ pound
Fish, fillets or steaks	⅓ to ½ pound
Fish, whole	¾ to 1 pound
Lobster, live	1 to 1½ pounds
Lobster meat	1½ pound yields 1 cup
Oysters, in the shell	½ dozen
Oysters, shucked	½ pint
Scallops	⅓ to ½ pound
Shrimp, cooked meat	⅓ to ½ pound
Shrimp, peeled and deveined	⅓ to ½ pound
Shrimp, raw and headless	½ to ⅔ pound

3. Choose a Great Recipe

This is the easy part now that you have this book. Here is a list of basic cooking methods for seafood.

Bake — usually at 350°
Broil — 4 inches from the heat source

Pan-fry — in ¼ inch of hot oil

Oven-fry — Bread the fish and use a 500° oven

Deep-fat Fry — Completely immersed in 375° oil

Poach — Completely covered with liquid (milk, water or
wine and selected seasonings)

Steam — In a deep pot with a tight cover and a rack

Bar-B-Q — Grill fish 4 inches from the hot coals.
Use a marinade or barbeque sauce.
(Recipes are included in this book.)

4. Don't Overcook Seafood

Timing is the most important secret to fabulous fish cookery. Fish is properly cooked when it turns opaque and flakes easily with a fork. Do not overcook fish or it will be dry and tough.

Ten Minute Rule: Measure the fish fillet or steak at its thickest part.

Allow ten minutes of cooking time per inch of thickness: If the fish measures less than one inch thick, shorten the cooking time slightly. Double the cooking time for fish that is still frozen. If you cook the fish in foil or in a sauce, allow an extra five minutes per inch.

Microwave: Yes! You can cook seafood in the microwave. The fish will be moist and delicious. Like the Ten Minute Rule above, use my **Three Minute Rule if using the microwave:** Allow approximately 3 minutes cooking time for every edible pound of fish.

Remember that the fish will continue cooking for a few minutes after microwaving. Even if the center is still a bit translucent, allow for this standing time. DO NOT OVERCOOK SEAFOOD!

☐ Rotate the dish during microwaving to insure an even distribution of heat.

☐ Seafood can be baked, boiled, poached, or steamed in your microwave.

☐ If your seafood is coated with a bread or crumb coating, cook it uncovered or it will become soggy (at the very most, cover with a loose paper towel.) Otherwise, cover your seafood dishes with plastic wrap. Be sure you allow the steam to escape; either turn back a corner or poke holes in the wrap.

If you are cooking more than one serving at a time, try to have the portions uniform in size. Fillets or steaks should be the same degree of thickness. When you cook more food, you must increase the cooking time.

7

One of the very best applications of the microwave is for reheating leftovers. Yesterday's crab cakes or steamed crab can be reheated without any loss of flavor or texture. It is truly amazing!

You can slip clams or mussels into the microwave and watch the shell open right before your eyes! It's magic!

Shrimp, crab, and lobster turn pink in a flash.

☐ Defrosting: Your microwave is a life saver when it comes to defrosting. In just a matter of minutes, the fish that was as hard as a rock, tucked away in your freezer from last summer, can be ready to prepare.

30% power — Low — Microwave for 6½ to 8½ minutes per pound.

50% power — Medium — Microwave 3 to 5 minutes per pound.

Other Tips to Fabulous Seafood Magic

☐ Keep your cooking methods and recipes simple.

☐ With chowders, make sure the amount of fish equals the amount of potatoes.

☐ Fish should always be kept as cool as possible. Since the quality of fish deteriorates very rapidly, try to pack it in ice; your goal is to keep it as close to 32° as you can.

☐ When you bring the fish home from the market, wash it, pat it dry with a paper towel, cover with a good plastic wrap (air right), and store it in the coldest part of your refrigerator.

☐ To freeze fish, place a meal size portion in a plastic bag. Fill the bag with cold water to completely cover the fish. Place it in a rigid metal pan the size of a bread pan and place in the freezer. Once frozen, the oblong package is removed from the pan and neatly stacked in your freezer compartment (put the pan back into your cupboard).

☐ Some seafood freezes better than others. These items freeze particularly well: scallops, soft shell crabs, crab meat and shad roe.

☐ For defrosting fish and seafood, look to step 4 of my Four Steps to Perfect Seafood under the microwave heading.

Chapter I — Hors D'Oeuvres

Broiled Crab Meltaways

It takes just 10 minutes to make these 48 hot canapes that melt in your mouth. Keeping a supply in your freezer takes little space, and you're always ready for unexpected guests. They also are excellent to serve with soup or a salad for a luncheon. I promise they'll be the talk of the evening.

Use 1 package of 6 English muffins. Slice in half and cut each half into fourths and arrange on two cookie trays. Put the following in the small bowl of your mixer:

½	*pound crab meat (or 1 7-ounce can)*
1	*stick margarine*
1	*7-ounce jar Old English sharp Cheddar cheese*
2	*tablespoons mayonnaise*
½	*teaspoon seasoned salt*
½	*teaspoon garlic salt*

Mix all this well. I use my mixer. Spread on English muffin quarters. Now, here's the secret — the most important step. You must freeze them at least 30 minutes. They may be kept frozen for weeks. When party time arrives, broil them until they puff up and are bubbly and slightly golden brown. They just take a few minutes. Serve hot and just listen to everyone carry on.

P.S. Watch them in the freezer. Someone at my house keeps stealing a few.

Shrimp Butter

This is a favorite of mine

1   8-ounce package cream cheese
1   stick butter
    juice of ½ lemon
1   onion, minced or grated
2   cups shrimp, cut up
    (I use the small fast-frozen kind)
4   tablespoons mayonnaise

Mix cheese and butter (it must be real butter) together until smooth. Add remaining ingredients and mix until blended. Garnish with extra whole shrimp. Serve with a bland cracker so your guests can appreciate the flavor.

Hot Crab Meat Spread

1   7½-ounce can fresh crab meat or
    6-ounce package frozen crab meat
1   8-ounce package cream cheese
3   tablespoons sherry or white wine
1   teaspoon horseradish
3   tablespoons minced onion
1   teaspoon Worcestershire sauce

Soften cream cheese and mix with remaining ingredients. Place in shallow pan (such as pretty pie plate) or 1-quart casserole. Sprinkle with paprika and bake at 350° until bubbly and light brown, about 15 minutes. Serve with crackers or toast. Can be made a day ahead and refrigerated until ready to reheat and serve.

Salmon Log

1	1-pound can salmon
1	8-ounce package cream cheese, room temperature
1	tablespoon lemon juice
2	teaspoons grated onion
1	teaspoon horseradish
¼	teaspoon Liquid Smoke
½	cup shopped pecans
3	tablespoons chopped parsley

Drain and flake salmon. Add next five ingredients and mix well, until smooth in texture. Chill several hours. Combine pecans with parsley; spread on sheet of waxed paper. Take half the salmon mixture and roll in nut mixture to form a small log. Chill. Serve with crackers or rye crisps. Makes 2 logs.

Best of Chesapeake Crab Spread

1	8-ounce package cream cheese, softened
¼	cup sour cream
3	tablespoons mayonnaise
1/8	teaspoon Accent
3	drops tabasco sauce
¼	teaspoon seasoned salt
8	ounces crab meat
2	ounces Cheddar cheese
	paprika

Mix first six ingredients well. Add 8 ounces crab meat and bake in shallow serving dish, such as a pretty pie pan, for 10 minutes at 350°. Take out of oven and sprinkle with 2 ounces of grated Cheddar cheese and paprika. Return to oven and bake until bubbly (about 15 minutes). Let stand 5 minutes. Serve with crackers.

Crab Mousse

2   3-ounce packages cream cheese
2   envelopes plain gelatin
2   10½-ounce cans tomato soup
2   medium green peppers, diced
2   bunches green onions, chopped
2   cups mayonnaise
2   teaspoons Worcestershire sauce
2   7½-ounce cans crab meat

Leave cream cheese at room temperature until very soft. Dissolve gelatin into soup. Bring soup to boil over low heat, stirring constantly until gelatin is dissolved. Pour small amount of hot soup over cream cheese and whisk with a wire whisk until smooth. Then add remaining soup, stirring constantly. Add mayonnaise, whisk again. Add remaining ingredients and mix well.

Pour into well-oiled fish mold. Decorate with olive and pimento strips after you unmold it onto platter. Serve with water wafers. Can be made several days ahead. If serving in muggy weather, add 1 more envelope of gelatin.

Dotty's Easy Cocktail Crab

2   pounds crab meat
15 ounces cream cheese
    almonds, toasted
2   tablespoons milk (approximately)
    salt and pepper

Mix softened cream cheese and milk, salt and pepper. Gently stir in the crab meat. Pour into a pretty pie plate or casserole dish. Bake until heated through at 325°, about 20 to 30 minutes. Garnish with toasted almonds and serve with bland crackers.

Chapter II — Sauces & Stuffings

Hollandaise Sauce

This classic sauce is so easy

3	egg yolks, room temperature
2	tablespoons lemon juice
1/8	teaspoon paprika
1/8	teaspoon cayenne pepper
¼	teaspoon salt
½	cup butter, melted

Double boiler method:

Mix egg yolks, lemon juice, paprika, cayenne pepper, and salt in top part of double boiler, using a wire whisk. When the egg yolks begin to thicken, very gradually add the melted butter. Keep mixing with the whisk constantly to prevent curdling.

Food processor method:

Put all the ingredients except the butter into the food processor, using the plastic or steel blade, mix briefly. Melt the butter until it just liquifies. Gradually, drip by drip, or a very slow thin stream, add the butter to the processor through the feed tube while the motor is running. Mix until smooth and thickened. Serve at once. Leftovers may be refrigerated.

An extra fancy twist: Make Mousseline Sauce by simply whipping equal parts of Hollandaise Sauce and whipping cream.

Sauce Mornay

½	cup grated Parmesan
½	cup heavy cream
1½	cups Sauce Veloute (see preceeding recipe)

Stir the Parmesan cheese into the Sauce Veloute until melted. Add the ½ cup heavy cream. Do not boil. Season with cayenne pepper and salt.

White Bechamel Sauce

This is a thick white sauce. Recipe yields 3½ cups. The sauce may be kept in the refrigerator for 2 or 3 days.

6	tablespoons butter
6	tablespoons flour
4½	cups hot milk
1	onion
1	clove garlic
1	teaspoon salt
¼	teaspoon finely ground white pepper
	dash nutmeg

Using a heavy saucepan, melt butter over high heat until it foams. Reduce heat to medium, add flour and cook the *roux* stirring hard and very constantly uncovered for 5 minutes. (You must cook the flour.) Remove the saucepan from the stove and add 1 cup hot milk stirring well and constantly to prevent sticking. Reduce heat to low, return pan to stove; add rest of the milk, 1 cup at a time, stirring constantly. Make a small slit in the onion and insert a whole clove of garlic. Drop in the onion (studded with garlic), and season with salt, pepper and nutmeg. Simmer over low heat uncovered for 30 minutes. Stir occasionally to prevent from sticking. Remove onion before serving.

Cocktail Sauce

½	cup catsup
½	cup chili sauce
	(all catsup may be used, if necessary)
1	tablespoon Worcestershire sauce
1	teaspoon garlic salt
1	tablespoon horseradish
	(this is a must, select hot or mild, to taste)
½	teaspoon dry mustard
½	teaspoon salt
1/8	teaspoon pepper, freshly ground

Mix all ingredients. Chill.

Bubbling Butter Sauce

This is a tasty sauce to brush on fish when broiling.

  1   *cup butter*
  2   *teaspoons Worcestershire sauce*
  2   *teaspoons prepared mustard*
  2   *tablespoons chili sauce*
  2   *drops tabasco*
  4   *teaspoons lemon juice*
  2   *tablespoons parsley, chopped*

Melt the butter and add all the ingredients. Heat until bubbly. Makes about 1¼ cups.

Tartar Sauce

No matter what the fish,
my husband has to have homemade tartar sauce.

  ½   *cup mayonnaise*
  2   *tablespoons grated dill pickle or*
      2 tablespoons sweet pickle relish
  ¼   *teaspoon Worcestershire sauce*
  1   *tablespoon finely grated raw onion or*
      ½ teaspoon onion powder

Mix all ingredients.

Sauce Veloute

2 tablespoons butter
2 tablespoons flour
1 cup fish stock

Combine the butter and flour in sauce pan. Cook until slightly brown in color. Stir in the fish stock and stir constantly until the sauce thickens. Simmer on very low heat for 10 minutes. Salt, pepper and herbs of your choice may be added.

Horseradish with Sour Cream Sauce

½ cup sour cream
1 tablespoon prepared horseradish
1 tablespoon catsup

Blend all ingredients and chill. This one is really a favorite of horseradish lovers!

Spicy Marinade

¼ cup margarine or butter
½ cup dry, white wine (or water)
½ teaspoon prepared mustard
½ teaspoon salt
¼ teaspoon lemon and pepper seasoning
¼ teaspoon seafood seasoning
1/8 teaspoon tarragon
1/8 teaspoon rosemary

Melt margarine or butter in a small pan. Add rest of ingredients and cook over low heat until seasonings are blended and mixture is warm. Makes about ¾ cupful of marinade.

Crab Meat Stuffing

½ cup crab meat
3 beaten eggs
2 tablespoons melted butter or margarine
1 tablespoon chopped onion
2 slices of bread, broken into chunks
  herbs or spices, to taste

Gently mix all ingredients.

Basic Bread Stuffing

Perfect for whole fish, fillets and lobster tails.

2 tablespoons butter or margarine
2 slices bread, broken into small chunks
¼ cup (or more) chopped onion
¼ cup (or more) chopped celery
1 egg, optional, as a binder
1 teaspoon fresh chopped parsley
½ teaspoon salt
1/8 teaspoon freshly ground black pepper, herbs or
  spices of your choice may be added, summer
  savory, thyme, rosemary, basil, ad infinitum

Melt butter in skillet. Add onion, celery, and seasonings. Saute until limp, but not browned. Add bread crumbs and egg. Stir lightly. Stuff whole fish lightly, or simply place over one fillet and put second fillet on top of the dressing.

Variation: Mushroom Dressing

Add mushrooms to the bread stuffing. Saute them with the celery and onion. Add a touch of soy sauce.

Chapter III — Fish

Flounder Rolls

Use 2 pounds fish fillets, any white fish, fresh or frozen. Soak fish in lemon juice and water while preparing filling.

Crab Meat Filling:

1	pound crab meat
½	onion, chopped
1	tablespoon mayonnaise
	Old Bay seasoning, to taste
1	tablespoon mustard
1	egg
	Worcestershire sauce, to taste
	salt and pepper
¼	green pepper, chopped

Combine ingredients, fill fillets, roll up — jellyroll fashion, and place in shallow baking dish.

White Wine and Mushroom Sauce:

1½	teaspoon salt
1	cup mushrooms, diced
2	tablespoons flour
2	tablespoons butter or margarine
1	cup skim milk
⅓ to ⅔	cup dry white wine
½	teaspoon crushed basil
	chopped parsley, to taste
	lemon and pepper seasoning
½	onion, chopped

Saute onion, mushrooms and margarine. Add milk and flour, cook until thickened. Add seasonings and wine and pour over fish rolls. Bake 35 to 55 minutes at 350° until fish flakes easily when tested with fork.

Stuffed Flounder

1	pound backfin crab meat
1	tablespoon butter
1	tablespoon flour
½	cup milk
1	teaspoon minced onion
1½	teaspoons Worcestershire sauce
2	slices white bread, cubed and crust removed
½	cup mayonnaise
1	tablespoon lemon juice
½	teaspoon salt
½	teaspoon pepper
2	tablespoons butter
2	pounds skinless flounder fillets
¼	cup butter
1	10¼-ounce can Newberg sauce
¼	cup milk

In medium pan, melt 1 tablespoon butter and blend in flour. Slowly add milk, stirring constantly. Cook, stirring, over medium heat until mixture comes to a boil and thickens. Mix in onion, Worcestershire sauce and bread cubes. Chill.

In another pan, melt 2 tablespoons butter until lightly browned. Add crab meat and toss; remove from heat.

Remove sauce from refrigerator and fold in mayonnaise, lemon juice, salt and pepper. Combine with crab meat.

Put 1 pound of flounder fillets in a 10 x 12 inch pan and spread stuffing on top. Put remaining fillets on top of stuffing, melt ¼ cup butter and pour over fillets.

Bake in 350° oven about 25 to 30 minutes.

In small saucepan, heat Newburg sauce, stirring in ¼ cup milk. Serve stuffed flounder on a bed of rice with Newburg sauce spooned on top.

Baked Red Snapper with Sour Cream Stuffing

3 or 4   *pounds dressed red snapper*
1½   *teaspoons salt*
      fresh lemon to squeeze
      sour cream stuffing (recipe follows)
2   *tablespoons melted fat or oil*

Clean, wash, and dry fish. Squeeze lemon juice inside and out. Sprinkle salt inside and out. Stuff the fish loosely with the dressing. Close the opening with small toothpicks or skewers. Place fish in well-greased baking dish. Brush with fat. Bake in moderate oven, 350°, for 40 to 60 minutes or until fish flakes easily when tested with a fork. Baste occasionally with fat. Remove skewers. Serves 6.

Sour Cream Stuffing

This tasty dressing may be used with other fish as well.

¾   *cup chopped celery*
½   *cup chopped onion*
¼   *cup melted fat or oil*
1   *quart dry bread cubes*
½   *cup sour cream*
¼   *cup diced peeled lemon*
2   *tablespoons grated lemon rind*
1   *teaspoon paprika*
1   *teaspoon salt*

Saute celery and onion in fat until tender. Combine all ingredients and mix lightly but thoroughly. Makes approximately 1 quart stuffing.

Fish Soup

    1   pound fish fillets (any white fish)
    ½   cup chopped bacon
    ½   cup chopped onion
    2   1-pound 12-ounce cans tomatoes
    2   cups diced potatoes
    1   cup catsup
    2   tablespoons Worcestershire sauce
    2   teaspoons salt
    ½   teaspoon celery seed
    ¼   teaspoon pepper

Skin fillets and cut into 1-inch pieces. Fry bacon until lightly browned. Add onion and cook until tender. Add tomatoes, potatoes, catsup and seasonings. Cook, covered, for 30 minutes, stirring occasionally. Add fish and continue cooking for 40 to 45 minutes, or until potatoes are tender. Serves 6.

Note: If your family doesn't love fish, open a window while cooking.

Captain Bob's World Famous Beer Batter

    3   eggs, beaten
 1½   cups flour
    3   tablespoons baking powder
    2   teaspoons salt
    1   teaspoon lemon pepper
    1   can beer, minus two medium swallows

This batter can be used to fry almost any fish. Cut fillets into small chunks, 1 to 2 inches. Coat chunks with beer sauce. Fry in 350° oil until the pieces float. May also coat fillets with the batter and fry in a small amount of hot oil. Turn and fry other side. This may be used with tremendous success with almost any kind of fish. Captain Bob has converted "fish haters" with this batter. It is especially outstanding with bluefish!.

Ben Florence's Famous Bass Chowder

1	cup chopped onion
2 to 3	slices bacon or
	½ cup diced salt pork
1	cup boiling water
2	cups diced raw potatoes
3 to 4	cups stewed tomatoes (1-pound can)
¼	cup catsup
2	tablespoons Worcestershire sauce
1/8	teaspoon thyme
1	teaspoon salt
½	teaspoon freshly ground pepper
2	cups (about 1 pound) diced fish fillets, such as striped bass, sea trout, haddock or cod

Saute onion until soft in drippings from bacon or pork. Add remaining ingredients, except fish; cover and simmer 20 to 30 minutes, or until potatoes are tender. Add fish; simmer 15 minutes and serve.

Hibachi Salmon

A change of pace for the summer bar-b-que.

1	salmon steak per serving
½	stick of butter per 2 servings
	garlic powder to taste

Melt the butter in a small sauce pan and add the garlic powder according to your tast (start with about ½ teaspoon). Grill the salmon steaks over a charcoal fire, basting regularly with the garlic butter. Turn the steak several times, the way you cook a hamburger, until each side is slightly charred.

Salmon with Olive-Rice Stuffing

6 to 8   pound salmon, dressed

Wash and dry fish thoroughly. Sprinkle inside of fish with salt and pepper and brush liberally with melted butter or margarine. Spoon olive-rice stuffing into fish and wrap in foil. Place wrapped fish in a shallow pan and bake in preheated 350° oven 15 to 18 minutes per pound, or until area near backbone is easily flaked, but moist. May also be prepared on the grill.

Stuffing:

½	*cup butter or margarine*
1½	*cups minced onion*
2	*cups diced celery*
2⅔	*cups cooked rice*
½	*teaspoon salt*
½	*teaspoon pepper*
½ to 1	*teaspoon ground sage, to taste*
½ to 1	*teaspoon thyme, to taste*
2	*cups stuffed olives, sliced*

Melt butter or margarine in skillet. Add onion and celery; saute until tender. Add rice and rest of ingredients. Season to taste after mixing well. Use to stuff whole salmon or as a side dish.

Broiled Swordfish

Many feel that swordfish
is unsurpassed in flavor and texture.

swordfish steak
lemon
butter
paprika

Spread the steak with butter and broil under the broiler for about 8 minutes on each side. Sprinkle with paprika and serve with lemon wedges.

Alternate: Spread the steak with mayonnaise and broil.

Swordfish Supreme

1	*pound swordfish, cut into pieces*
½	*pound fresh mushrooms, sliced*
1	*green pepper, cut in rings or strips*
1	*onion, sliced into rings*
½	*cup olive oil*
¼	*teaspoon salt*
1/8	*teaspoon pepper*
¼	*teaspoon oregano*
¼	*teaspoon paprika*
1	*can anchovies*

Saute the mushrooms, green pepper and onion in the olive oil. Add the swordfish and brown. Add the seasonings and anchovies. Cover the pan and steam for 10 minutes. Serves 3 to 4.

Shark Steaks Hawaiian

     4   shark steaks, 1 inch thick
    1/8 pound butter
     ¼   teaspoon salt
    1/8 teaspoon pepper
     8   ounces canned pineapple rings
     4   teaspoons coconut chips or shredded coconut

Melt the butter in a skillet. Brown the steaks on each side in the butter. Add the juice from the can of pineapple. Cover tightly and steam for 5 minutes. Place a pineapple ring on top of each steak and steam for 5 more minutes. Serve with 1 teaspoon of coconut chips on each steak. This recipe can also be used with bonita, haddock, cod or striped bass.

Bluefish Cakes

Any fish may be used in this recipe, such as striped bass, weakfish or sea trout.

     1   pound flaked, cooked fish*
     6   saltine crackers, broken semifine
         salt, to taste
     1   heaping teaspoon Old Bay Seasoning
     1   teaspoon celery seed
     1   heaping tablespoon parsley, finely chopped
     1   egg
     2   tablespoons salad dressing

Mix all dry ingredients; add to the flaked fish. Blend egg and salad dressing and add to mixture. Handle very gently. Shape into patties a little larger than saltines. Fry in ¼-inch hot oil at 380° until light golden brown. Serve with saltines, prepared mustard and creamy cole slaw.

*When using bluefish, discard dark meat while flaking. This is important; the dark meat and skin have a strong taste.

Basic Baked Fish

Any type of fish fillet or fish steak may be baked in this manner. Preheat oven to 475-500° while making sauce.

Sauce:

> 2   *tablespoons butter*
> 1   *tablespoon lemon juice*
> 1   *tablespoon Worcestershire sauce*
> ½   *teaspoon paprika*

Baste the fish with sauce. Oily or "stronger" fish may be seasoned further with any commercial seafood seasoning. Bluefish is particularly good this way.

Bake the fish in a single layer in a shallow pan for:

6 to 7 minutes for fish ½-inch thick;

7 to 9 minutes for fish ¾-inch thick.

Remove from oven as soon as fish whitens inside and begins to flake when fork-tested. Above all, do not overcook.

Bass Teriyaki on the Outdoor Grill

Teriyaki sauce for marinade

¼	*cup dry sherry*
¼	*cup soy sauce*
2	*tablespoons dry onion soup mix*
2	*tablespoons brown sugar*

Prepare the barbecue grill by putting foil over the grate and punching several holes through foil with a fork.

Before cooking, marinate the striped bass or other white-flesh fish fillets or steaks 10 to 20 minutes, according to thickness of fish. Marinating for a shorter rather than a longer time is preferable.

Place the marinated fillets on the foiled grill, turning once and removing as soon as fish flakes when fork-tested. I have used this recipe very successfully indoors with the broiler.

Bluefish Surprise

Broil 1 pound of bluefish fillets for 7-10 minutes, skin side down. I squeeze on lemon juice and add little pats of butter before broiling. Cool, flake.

1	cup soft bread crumbs
1	cup mayonnaise or salad dressing
¾	cup milk
6	hard-cooked eggs, chopped
¼	cup sliced, stuffed green olives
¾	teaspoon salt
	dash of pepper
⅓	cup chopped onion
½	cup buttered, soft bread crumbs

Mix all ingredients (including fish), except buttered crumbs. Place in greased individual bakers or into a 1 quart casserole. Top with buttered bread crumbs. Bake in moderate oven at 350° for 20-25 minutes or until hot throughout. Trim with stuffed olive slices. Makes 6 servings.

This recipe is easy to double for a crowd. Doubled with 1 large bluefish and just the 6 eggs. It fills my 13 x 9 inch pan. The surprise is the bluefish. No one believes that I caught it myself.

The recipe can feature crabmeat or any white fish you happen to have.

Chef's Pickled Herring (Glasmastarsill)

Traditionally a part of the smorgasbord, pickled herring is an integral part of the Swedish Christmas celebration.

2   *large salt herring*
½   *tablespoon whole allspice, crushed*
2   *bay leaves*
1½   *whole ginger slices (fresh ginger is now available in local groceries, or use ground ginger to taste)*
½   *teaspoon mustard seed*
1   *small piece horseradish, diced*
2   *red onions, sliced*
½   *carrot, sliced*

Dressing:

1   *cup white vinegar*
⅓   *cup water*
½   *cup sugar*

Clean fish, removing heads, and soak overnight in cold water. Drain well on absorbent paper. Cut crosswise in half-inch slices and place together with dry ingredients, onions and carrots in large glass jar. (Use old mayonnaise, peanut butter or other jars.)

Mix vinegar, water and sugar; bring to boiling point. Chill. Then pour over herring in jars and let stand overnight in refrigerator. Always serve from the jar. Red onions and bright carrots make this a colorful dish.

Chapter IV — Crabs

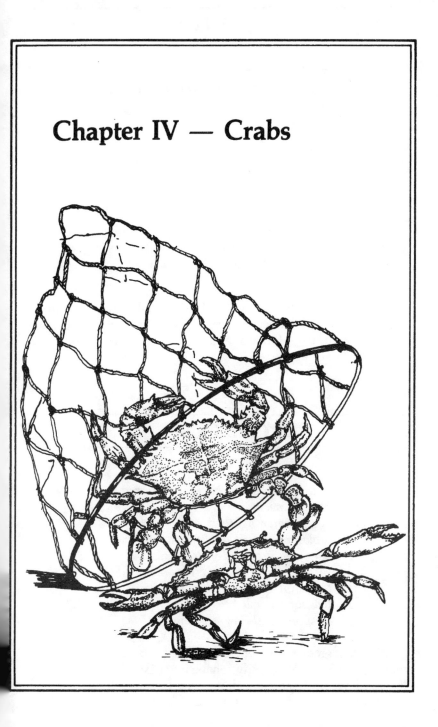

Crab Louis

1   small head lettuce
2   cups fresh crab meat (about 1 pound)
4   hard-cooked eggs
2   tomatoes, quartered
1   medium cucumber, sliced

Louis Dressing:

⅓   cup mayonnaise
½   cup bottled chili sauce
2   tablespoons French dressing
½   teaspoon minced onion
½   teaspoon Worcestershire sauce
    salt and pepper

Mix dressing ingredients until blended (makes about 1 cup).
Place shredded lettuce on salad plate. Top with crab meat. Garnish with egg, tomato and cucumber. Serve with Louis dressing. Serves 4.

Crab Cakes

1   pound crab meat, backfin preferred
    but not necessary
2   eggs, beaten lightly
2   tablespoons best quality mayonnaise
1   teaspoon prepared yellow mustard
2   slices day old bread, crusts removed
1   teaspoon Worcestershire sauce
1   teaspoon parsley
½   teaspoon Old Bay seasoning

Mix all ingredients except crab in large bowl. Add carefully picked crab meat. Mix gently. Shape into cakes. Refrigerate for at least ½ hour (not necessary, but makes them much easier to fry). Fry in small amount oil or butter until browned on each side.

Crab Meat in Shell Soup

¼　cup chopped onion
¼　cup chopped green pepper
¼　cup diced celery
2　tablespoons butter
2　13¾-ounce cans chicken broth
1　7½-ounce can tomatoes
¼　cup tiny macaroni shells
2　potatoes, cut in small pieces
1　tablespoon parsley
¼　teaspoon salt
½　pound crab meat, picked

In large saucepan, cook onion, green pepper and celery in butter until tender. Add broth, tomatoes, macaroni shells, potatoes, parsley, salt and pepper; bring to boiling. Cover and simmer 30 minutes. Add crab meat; cook 5 minutes longer. Makes 6 servings.

Crab Imperial

3　pounds crab meat (backfin)
1　green pepper, diced finely
　　(optional, parboil or omit entirely)
½　jar red pimento, diced finely
1½　teaspoon salt
½　teaspoon white pepper
2　raw eggs
1　cup mayonnaise
1　tablespoon dry mustard

Mix all ingredients together and toss crab meat into mixture last. Break recipe down to ⅓ of amount to serve 3 people. 1 pound of crab meat serves 3 heaping portions. Heap in crab shells or large casserole dish. Top with mayonnaise and paprika. Bake at 350° for 20 minutes until top is brown. Serve hot or cold.

Dr. Srsic's Maryland Crab Soup

The soup base is best made the day before and refrigerated overnight:

1	large soup pot (about 2 gallon size)
1	ham bone
2	pounds top sirloin roast beef, cut into small pieces
1	onion, medium, diced
4	14-ounce cans Italian tomatoes, blended in blender
1	gallon water or more if necessary to cover ham bone

Simmer gently about 4 hours or until beef is tender. Refrigerate overnight. This forces the fat from the ham bone to the top of the liquid so that it may easily be skimmed off the next day. Remove all bits of ham, bone and cartilage with a slotted spoon and discard.

The next day add: 12 blue crabs*, medium to large size, live.

1	head cabbage, shredded
10	small potatoes, raw, diced into small pieces
1	can tomato sauce (large)
2 to 4	teaspoons Old Bay seasoning
6	beef bouillon cubes
10	chicken bouillon cubes
2	strips bacon
1	teaspoon paprika
1/4	pound butter
8	fresh peeled tomatoes, put through blender
1	large bag frozen lima beans
1	large bag frozen peas
1	large bag frozen corn
2	large bags frozen assorted soup vegetables

Add water to nearly top of the soup pot and simmer until all vegetables are tender, about $1^1/_2$-2 hours.

---

*To clean crabs live: put lots of ice over crabs, which numbs them and makes them easy to handle. Remove large claws and crack in 2 places with a nutcracker. Add to soup base. Remove legs, shell and dead-man fingers and discard. Break rest of crab in half and add to soup base.

Cream of Crab Soup

  2   pounds crab meat
  1   vegetable bouillon cube
  1   cup boiling water
  ¼   cup chopped onion
  ¼   cup butter
  2   tablespoons flour
  1   teaspoon salt
  ¼   teaspoon celery salt
1/8   teaspoon pepper
  1   tablespoon hot sauce (tabasco)
  1   quart milk
  2   tablespoons cornstarch
       dried parsley flakes for garnish

Remove cartilage from crab meat. Dissolve bouillon cube in water.

In 4-quart saucepan, cook onion in butter until tender. Blend in flour and seasonings.

Add milk, bouillon and cornstarch gradually and cook over medium heat, stirring constantly, until mixture is thick enough to coat the spoon. Add crab meat; heat, but do not boil. Garnish with parsley flakes.

Note: Soup tastes better if prepared the day before serving.

Corn and Crab Soup

  2   cups chicken stock
  1   can sweet corn (cream style)
  2   eggs
  1   tablespoon sherry
  ½   teaspoon salt
  1   teaspoon cornstarch,
         mixed with 1 tablespoon water
½ to 1   pound crab meat (claw)

Bring stock and corn to boil. Add beaten eggs and cook 1 minute. Add sherry, salt and cornstarch mixture. Stir well; add crab meat. Simmer until crab is heated. Serves 4.

Hot Crab Fondue

1   pound crab meat
1   8-ounce package cream cheese
6   ounces Monterey Jack cheese, grated
½   cup milk
¼   cup sherry
1   teaspoon lemon juice
    salt and pepper
    French bread, cut into cubes

Mix all ingredients except bread. Heat 5 to 10 minutes in fondue pot or bake in a shallow dish 20 minutes at 350°. Dip bread cubes into fondue and enjoy.

Leftovers may be frozen and reheated later at 350° for 25 to 30 minutes.

Seafood Newburg Deluxe

1   pound backfin crab meat
½   pound cooked, shelled shrimp
4   tablespoons butter
4   tablespoons flour
½   pint cream
4 to 5   tablespoons dry sherry
¾   cup grated sharp Cheddar cheese
1   4-ounce can mushrooms
    salt and pepper to taste

Make a cream sauce with the butter, flour and cream. Add salt, pepper and sherry. Remove from heat and add crab meat, shrimp and mushrooms. Pour the mixture into a buttered casserole or individual baking dishes. Sprinkle with grated cheese and cook in a 350° oven, about 20 minutes, until cheese melts and sauce is bubbly. Do not overcook. Serves 4 to 6.

World Famous St. Mary's Crab Soup

Served at Maryland Seafood Festival

  1   *beef soup bone*
  3   *quarts water*
 24   *ounces V-8 juice*
  1   *pound canned tomatoes*
  2   *pounds claw crab meat, fresh, hand-picked*
        (note directions; each pound is added separately)
  1   *tablespoon salt*
 ½   *teaspoon black pepper*
  1   *tablespoon Old Bay seasoning*
  1   *large onion, chopped*
  1   *large green pepper, chopped*
  2   *stalks celery, chopped*
  4   *potatoes, peeled and cubed*
  1   *20-ounce package frozen mixed vegetables*
3 to 5 *good shakes Worcestershire sauce*

In big soup pot, put beef bone, V-8 juice, water and 1 pound crab meat. Add seasonings, green pepper, onion and celery. Simmer 1½ to 2 hours. Then add potatoes and frozen mixed vegetables. Cook until potatoes are tender, 20 to 30 minutes. Wait until a half-hour before serving time to add the last pound of crab meat.

Leftovers are even better the next day. A word of caution: You must be constantly careful when cooking with crab meat. Cool soup thoroughly and refrigerate immediately. This will last one to two days in refrigerator or may be frozen for longer storage.

Crab Stuffed Chicken Breasts

6   chicken breasts, skinned and boned
½   cup chopped onions
½   cup chopped celery
3   tablespoons butter or margarine
½   teaspoon paprika
1   envelope Hollandaise sauce mix
¾   cup milk
3   tablespoons dry, white wine
1   7-ounce can crab meat, drained, or fresh crab
½   cup herb seasoned stuffing mix
2   tablespoons all purpose flour
2   tablespoons dry, white wine
½   cup (2 ounces) shredded Swiss cheese

Pound chicken to flatten. Sprinkle with a little salt and pepper. Cook onion and celery in the 3 tablespoonfuls of butter until tender. Remove from heat; add the 3 tablespoonfuls of wine, the crab and stuffing mix. Toss. Divide mixture among the chicken breasts. Roll up tightly and secure with skewers or string.

Combine flour and paprika. Coat chicken. Place in a 11¾ x 7½ x 1¾ inch baking dish. Drizzle with 2 tablespoonfuls of melted butter. Bake uncovered in 375° oven for 1 hour. Transfer to platter. Blend sauce mix and milk. Cook and stir until thick. Add remaining wine and cheese. Stir until cheese melts. Pour some on chicken. Pass the remaining in a sauce boat. Serves 6.

Crab Souffle Casserole

    2   7¼-ounce cans crab meat or
        1 pound frozen crab meat or fresh crab meat
    8   slices bread
    ½   cup mayonnaise
    1   cup chopped celery
    1   green pepper, chopped
    1   medium onion, chopped
    ½   teaspoon salt
    4   eggs, slightly beaten
    3   cups milk
    1   10½-ounce can cream of mushroom soup
    ½   cup shredded Cheddar cheese

Drain and cut crab meat into chunks. Dice half the bread into bottom of large, buttered casserole. Combine crab, mayonnaise, celery, green pepper, onion and salt. Spread over diced bread. Trim crusts from remaining bread, dice and place over crab mixture. Mix eggs and milk together and pour over bread. Cover and refrigerate for several hours or overnight. Bake at 325° for 15 minutes. Remove from oven and spoon undiluted mushroom soup over top; sprinkle with shredded cheese. Return to oven and bake for 1 hour longer.

Yield: 8-10 servings.

Note: I add ½ cupful of slivered blanched almonds. And sometimes I add a can of water chestnuts, drained and sliced. These are added with the other vegetables and stirred in. This recipe really is delicious with canned crab meat. Try it once.

Hot Crab Meat Salad

1   large, green pepper, finely chopped
1   small onion, finely chopped
1   cup celery, finely chopped
1   pound crab meat, shredded and shells removed
    (claw or backfin)
1   cup mayonnaise
½   teaspoon salt
1   teaspoon Worcestershire sauce
1   pinch of black pepper
1   cup cooked shrimp, deveined and chopped coarsely
1   cup bread crumbs, mixed with
    2 tablespoons melted butter

Combine pepper, onion, celery and all other ingredients except
bread crumbs. Bake in glass casserole dish, uncovered, topping
with bread crumb-butter mixture at 350° until brown on top,
about 25 minutes. Serves about 6 people.

Crab Quiche

1   unbaked pie shell
1   cup natural Swiss cheese, shredded (4 ounces)
3   beaten eggs
1   cup light cream
¼   teaspoon dry mustard
¼   cup sliced almonds
½   pound crab meat
2   green onions, chopped with tops
½   teaspoon grated lemon peel
    dash of mace
1   teaspoon salt

Sprinkle cheese evenly over bottom of pie shell. Top with crab
meat, sprinkle with green onion. Combine eggs, cream, salt,
lemon peel, dry mustard and mace. Pour over crab meat. Top
with almonds. Bake in slow oven at 325° about 55 minutes or until
set. Remove from oven and let stand for 10 minutes before
serving.

Chapter V — Oysters

The Oyster is Our Pearl

Marilyn Latham, the former home economist for the Maryland Seafood Marketing Authority, Department of Economic and Community Development, has a story to share about Maryland's pride, the oyster. Indeed, the oyster is our pearl.

"This is a primer of oysters for the newcomer, with a few tips for the seafood gourmet.

Oysters on the half shell are a delicacy the world over, traditionally served on cracked ice with cocktail sauce, horseradish, lemon and oyster crackers. Use small forks or toothpicks and allow at least 6 per person. Once you've jumped this hurdle, you'll know whether or not raw oysters are your dish. The larger the oyster, the more expensive, and the vocabulary follows:

Extra Selects — about 16 to 20 a pint
Selects — about 20 to 25 a pint
Standards — 25 to 35 a pint
Smalls — more than 35 a pint
Counts — for institutional use, elegant restaurants, clubs, hotels, fewer than 16 a pint

The standards and smalls are used more for stews and chowders, bisques and fritters. Market forms include live in the shell, fresh shucked, frozen shucked, frozen breaded and canned."

Waveland Oysters

1   *dozen select oysters, in the shell*
1   *cup grated Cheddar cheese*
½   *small onion, chopped fine*
½   *cup slivered almonds*
½   *cup bacon bits*
     enough mayonnaise to cover

Shuck oysters. Clean and dry them. Return to their shells or put into individual ramekins. In a bowl, combine other ingredients. Spread each oyster with some of the mixture. Broil for 5 minutes, or until cheese bubbles. Garnish with fresh parsley. Serves 4 as an appetizer.

Oysters Rockefeller

24	oysters in shells
2	tablespoons onion, chopped
2	tablespoons butter, melted
2	tablespoons fresh parsley, chopped
1/8	teaspoon paprika
	salt
	pepper
1	cup cooked spinach, chopped fairly fine
¼	cup fine dry bread crumbs
½	cup butter or margarine
	rock salt

You may use shucked oysters and assemble this dish in small baking shells. This eliminates the time required to open 24 oysters.

Open the oysters with an oyster knife. Remove the oysters from their shells, drain very well. Wash the shells. Place each oyster in the deep half of the shell.

Combine parsley, onion, and the melted butter. Spread this over each oyster. Sprinkle each one with a little salt, pepper and paprika. Top each with 2 teaspoons spinach, then ½ teaspoon bread crumbs. Dot each one with butter (about 1 teaspoon each). Arrange your Oysters Rockefeller on a bed of rock salt in a shallow pan. Bake at 450° until browned, about 10 minutes. Serves 8.

Mrs. O'Berry's Oysters Casino

1	pint shucked oysters
4	slices bacon, chopped
1	small onion, chopped
1	small stalk celery, chopped
1	teaspoon lemon juice
¾	teaspoon salt
1/8	teaspoon pepper
8	drops Worcestershire sauce
4	drops hot sauce

Drain oysters and arrange in single layer in shallow baking dish. Partially fry bacon. Add onion and celery to skillet and saute until tender. Remove from heat and add lemon juice and seasonings.

Spread bacon mixture over oysters. Bake at 400° about 10 to 15 minutes, until edges curl.

Excellent appetizer served with saltines or small squares of melba toast.

Optional: You may add 1/8 to ¼ teaspoon Old Bay seasoning if you wish.

Tidewater Tacos

2 dozen shucked select oysters (about 1 pint)
1 cup cracker meal
1 tablespoon chili powder
½ teaspoon salt
1 egg
  shredded Monterey Jack cheese
1 cup milk
  hot oil or shortening for frying
1 dozen taco shells
  shredded lettuce
  chopped fresh tomatoes
  minced jalapeno peppers (optional)

Drain oysters and pat dry. Mix cracker meal, chili powder and salt. Beat egg and milk together. Heat oil or shortening in skillet to between 350° and 375°. Dip oysters in egg mixture and roll in seasoned crumbs. Fry in hot fat 3 to 5 minutes. (Oysters can be deep fat fried or shallow fat fried, turning once during cooking.) Drain oysters on paper towels after removing from fryer. Place 2 fried oysters on each taco shell; dress with lettuce, tomatoes, peppers and cheese. Makes 1 dozen.

Cheese, Eggs and Oysters Brunch

Second Place, Chesapeake Appreciation Days

1 pound Cheddar cheese, grated
1 dozen eggs
1 teaspoon Old Bay seasoning
1 pint oysters, drained

Beat eggs well with Old Bay seasoning, or mix in blender. Butter a 9 x 13 inch ovenproof dish and cover the bottom with half the grated cheese. Pour in the beaten eggs carefully. Place oysters on eggs in an even layer. Top with remainder of grated cheese. Bake at 350° for 30 to 40 minutes, or until golden. May be served hot as a main dish or in small cubes (cold) as an hors d'oeuvres.

Oysters a la Garvey

'Tis the season for oysters!

1	cup oysters
1	cup cooked mushrooms
1½	cups milk
3	tablespoons flour
½	teaspoon salt
3	tablespoons butter
1	teaspoon onion juice
½	teaspoon lemon juice
2	egg yolks or 1 egg
	patty shells

Place oysters in hot pan. Cook in butter until edges curl. Make sauce with juice from oysters, adding enough milk to equal 2 cups. Thicken with flour. Cook 2 to 4 minutes. Add sauteed mushrooms, lemon juice, onion juice and salt. Beat egg and add to hot mixture, very slowly at first, combine carefully. Add oysters. Cook in double boiler over hot water until thick. Serve over prepared patty shells.

Note: If you choose to use fresh mushrooms, saute them first in 2 tablespoons butter.

Chapter VI — Shrimp

Sweet and Sour Shrimp

2   pounds raw peeled shrimp, large size
2   tablespoons red wine
4   tablespoons soy sauce
4   tablespoons flour
2   tablespoons cornstarch
    oil to deep fry
3   green peppers, quartered
1   onion (4 ounces), quartered
1   carrot (4 ounces),
    cut into wedges and boiled for 8 minutes
4   ounces water chestnuts
4   slices pineapple, cut up
5   tablespoons oil
12 tablespoons sugar
8   tablespoons soy sauce
2   tablespoons wine
4   tablespoons vinegar
8   tablespoons tomato sauce
2   tablespoons cornstarch mixed with ½ cup water

Mix shrimp with wine, soy sauce, flour and 2 tablespoons cornstarch. Fry shrimp in deep oil for 1 to 2 minutes. Turn out on plate.

Saute green peppers, onion, carrot, water chestnuts, and pineapple in 5 tablespoons oil.

Mix sugar, 8 tablespoons soy sauce, wine, vinegar and tomato sauce in bowl and add to sauteed ingredients. When mixture boils up, add the cornstarch mixture, stirring constantly. Add shrimp and mix well. Serve hot!

Shrimp, Tomato and Cheese Pie

1½	pounds shrimp, cooked and peeled
2	tablespoons basil
3	tablespoons chives
3	cloves garlic
½	cup parsley, chopped
½	teaspoon salt
1/8	teaspoon pepper
½	onion, chopped
½	green pepper, chopped
½	pound butter
1	whole egg
2	egg yolks
½	cup mayonnaise
1	pound Jarlsberg cheese, grated
4	tomatoes, cut into chunks
1	11-inch pie crust, unbaked (may be purchased)
	bread crumbs
	paprika, to sprinkle

Saute basil, chives, garlic, parsley, salt, pepper, onion and green pepper in butter until limp. In a large bowl mix together eggs, yolks and mayonnaise. Add shrimp and vegetables and mix well. Pour into pastry-lined pan, sprinkle with bread crumbs and paprika. Bake for 45 minutes at 350°.

Crust:

1½	cups flour
¼	pound butter
	small amount of water
	dash salt

Mix flour and butter until mixture resembles cornmeal. Pour in a bit of water and dash of salt and stir. Place on pastry cloth and roll out. Yields one 11-inch or two 7-inch pie shells.

Chinese Shrimp

2	tablespoons vegetable oil
1	small onion, chopped
1	teaspoon grated ginger root
4 to 5	cloves garlic, minced
5 to 6	Chinese dried black mushrooms, soaked 30 minutes in warm water and sliced (regular fresh mushrooms may be used)
1	cup peas, fresh or frozen (defrosted)
1	pound shrimp, just barely cooked and peeled
½	cup chicken broth (may use bouillon)
2	tablespoons soy sauce
1	teaspoon salt

Mix 1 tablespoon cornstarch in 2 tablespoons water, set aside. Heat oil in wok and stir-fry onion, ginger and garlic for 1 to 2 minutes. Add mushrooms and peas and stir-fry 1 to 2 minutes. Combine broth, soy sauce, salt and cornstarch mixture. Add to wok and heat until sauce boils and has thickened. Serve immediately over boiled rice.

Shrimp De Jonghe

1¼	pounds cooked, shelled shrimp
1	stick butter, melted
½	cup dry white wine
⅓	cup snipped parsley
1/8	teaspoon garlic powder
2	cups soft bread crumbs
½	teaspoon paprika
	dash cayenne

Place shrimp in baking dish in a single layer. Combine remaining ingredients and spread over shrimp. Bake about 25 minutes at 350°.

Shrimp Harpin

Serves 6-8

2	pounds larger fresh shrimp
1	tablespoon fresh, frozen or bottled lemon juice
3	tablespoons salad oil
¾	raw regular or processed rice
2	tablespoons butter or margarine
¼	cup green pepper, minced
¼	cup onion, minced
1	teaspoon salt
1/8	teaspoon pepper
1/8	teaspoon mace
	dash of pepper
1	can condensed tomato soup, undiluted
½	cup heavy cream
½	cup slivered almonds
½	cup sherry
	paprika

Early in the day, shell, clean and cook shrimp in boiling, salted water for 5 minutes and drain. Place in 2 quart casserole. Sprinkle with lemon juice and oil. Meanwhile, cook rice as package directs. Drain. Chill all.

About 70 minutes before serving, put butter into skillet, and saute green pepper and onion for 5 minutes. To shrimp in casserole, add onion mixture, rice, salt and rest of ingredients except ¼ cupful of the almonds and paprika. Top with reserved almonds and sprinkle with paprika. Bake in 350° oven (preheated) until bubbly which is about 30 minutes.

Shrimp Casserole

6   slices of bread, broken into bits
½   pound sharp Cheddar cheese, broken up
½   teaspoon dry mustard
3   eggs, beaten
1   pound cooked shrimp
     (do not overcook shrimp, it is going to be baked)
¼   cup margarine, melted
     salt to taste
1   pint milk

Layer shrimp, bread and cheese bits in a greased 3 quart casserole. Pour melted butter over mixture. Beat eggs, add mustard, salt and milk. Mix well and pour over ingredients in casserole. Place in refrigerator and let stand a minimum of 3 hours, or overnight. Cook, covered, in a preheated 350° oven for 1 hour. This casserole may be made without that expensive pound of shrimp by substituting a similar seafood, langustino.

Shrimp Fried Rice

½   cup chopped onion
½   cup chopped green pepper
¼   cup oil or butter
3   cups cold cooked rice
2   eggs, lightly beaten
2   tablespoons soy sauce
¼   teaspoon black pepper
2   teaspoons beef bouillon granules
2   cups shrimp or other cooked seafood or meat
     (chicken, lobster, pork or beef)

Saute onion in hot oil until golden brown. Stir in beaten eggs, green pepper, black pepper, bouillon and soy sauce. Saute 3 minutes, stirring often. Add rice; heat thoroughly, still stirring. Add shrimp and continue heating until mixture is steaming hot.

This is a great way to use leftover rice and meat. A stir-fry meal, delicious and easy to prepare, is a pleasant change of pace.

Chapter VII — Scallops, Clams & Other Delicacies

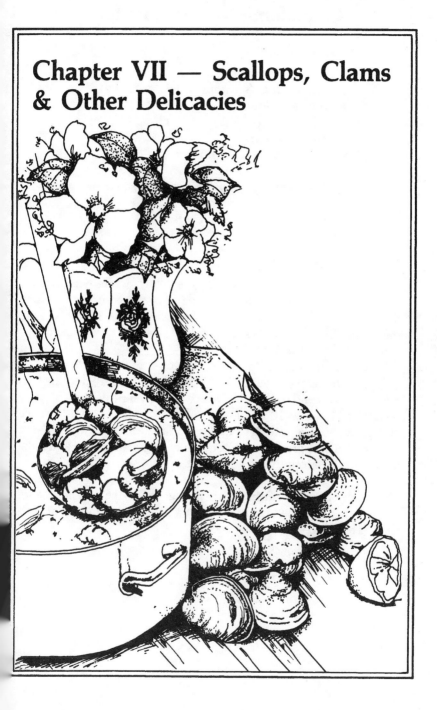

Coquilles St. Jacques (Scallops)

1   pound raw scallops
2   dry shallots (scallions) finely chopped
4   ounces dry white wine
4   ounces water
½   teaspoon salt
1/8   teaspoon freshly ground white pepper
1   cup hot white sauce
     (see White Bechamel Sauce in chapter on sauces)
     dash cayenne pepper
2   tablespoons heavy cream
¼   cup grated Gruyere cheese

In a saute pan, combine scallops, shallots, white wine, water, salt and pepper. Cover with buttered foil or waxed paper, pressing the foil with your fingers until it meets the surface of ingredients, then bring liquid to boil on a high heat. Reduce heat to medium, simmer scallops for 5 minutes.

Take scallops out of liquid and put on a heated platter.

Reduce remaining liquid by 2/3 over high heat. Reduce heat to medium and blend in the white sauce and cayenne pepper. Simmer uncovered for 8 to 10 minutes. Add scallops and cream to sauce and pour mixture into 4 Coquille St. Jacques shells. (I use large scallop shells.) Sprinkle each coquille with grated cheese and bake under broiler around 8 to 10 minutes.

Optional: before putting everything into the shells, saute mushrooms, chopped finely, and put a layer in the bottom of each shell. Then add everything else.

Baked Scallops

1½ pounds scallops
½ stick butter
½ cup dry bread crumbs
½ teaspoon salt
1/8 teaspoon freshly ground black pepper
¼ teaspoon paprika

Defrost scallops and wipe dry. Place in a shallow baking dish in single layer. Melt ½ stick butter and pour over the scallops. Sprinkle with ½ cup dry breadcrumbs, salt, pepper, and paprika. Cover and bake in preheated 375° oven for 10 minutes. Uncover and bake another 5 minutes or until brown.

Deviled Scallops

1 pound scallops
2 tablespoons butter, melted
½ teaspoon dry mustard
½ teaspoon celery salt
1 tablespoon lemon juice
2 tablespoons butter, melted
1 clove garlic, minced
2 tablespoons flour
2 teaspoons horseradish
2 tablespoons chopped parsley
1/8 teaspoon freshly ground black pepper
½ cup soft bread crumbs

Chop scallops. Saute garlic in butter a few minutes; blend in flour and seasonings. Add scallops and cook 4 to 5 minutes, stirring constantly. Place into six well greased, individual shells. Combine butter and crumbs, sprinkle over top of each shell. Bake in moderate oven, 350°, 15 to 20 minutes, or until brown. Serves 6.

Clams Casino

1   *stick margarine*
1   *stalk celery, minced finely*
1   *onion, minced finely*
1   *clove garlic, minced finely*
30 *fresh clams, steamed, chopped fine or*
     2 6½-ounce cans minced clams

Saute celery, onion and garlic in 1 stick of margarine for 10 minutes. Do not allow this to brown. Pour in 30 fresh clams, chopped or 2 6½-ounce cans minced clams, juice and all. Add in same skillet:

1   *whole egg*
2   *teaspoons salt*
1   *tablespoon flour*
¼   *teaspoon pepper*
¼   *teaspoon thyme (don't omit this; it adds a lot)*
2   *tablespoons chopped parsley*
    dash tabasco sauce
1   *tablespoon Worcestershire sauce*
2   *tablespoons chili sauce*

Add ½ cupful of white cracker crumbs. It should be the consistency of oatmeal. If it is too runny, add more crumbs. Fill clam half shells. (I save my shells and wash them in the dishwasher.) Sprinkle with bread crumbs and paprika. Bake at 400° for 10 minutes until bubbly. Serve warm on a small plate with a small fork. These could be served as a fish course in the dining room. I have put the mixture into larger scallop shells and served them as the main event for a luncheon. If they are frozen, defrost for about 1 hour before baking.

Paella

Meats:

- ½   pound chicken — thighs, legs,
      cut into bite size pieces
- ½   pound sausage, cut into bite size pieces
- ½   pound pork, use center cut chops,
      cut out meat into bite size pieces
- ½   pound haddock fish fillets
      (other white fish may be used)
- ½   pound shrimp, with shells
- 1   dozen small clams, with shells

Vegetables:

- 1   green pepper
- 2   large ripe tomatoes
- ½   pound frozen peas
- 1   onion
      canned pimentos
      parsley
- 1   cup rice

Spices:

- ¼   teaspoon cinnamon
- 1   teaspoon paprika
- 1   bay leaf
- 1   teaspoon salt
- ¼   teaspoon dark red ground saffron
- 2   garlic cloves, crushed

(continued on next page)

Boil chicken in water for 30 minutes. In very large skillet, lightly greased with olive oil, fry for about 15 minutes, the boiled chicken, sausage and pork. Add slices green pepper, haddock and shrimp and fry together with meat for 5 minutes. Add more olive oil if needed. Add 1 cup rice, mixing thoroughly with meats. Add clams, scrubbed and dried, with shells. They'll open as they heat. Keep on low heat.

In a separate saucepan, heat ½ cup olive oil, chop in tomatoes and onion. Add cinnamon, paprika, bay leaf, 1 teaspoon salt, saffron and 2 cups boiling water; mix thoroughly. Add peas and cook over medium high heat for 10 minutes. Add above mixture to skillet slowly. Reserve small amount of liquid. Add pimentos and cook for 10 more minutes or until rice is soft. Meanwhile, mix garlic cloves with 1 tablespoon parsley, chopped. Add reserved liquid to make a paste. Add to skillet, stirring in and cooking for 10 minutes or more until all liquid is absorbed by the rice. By now the saffron will turn the rice yellow and the haddock has flaked into the rice. Let stand for 5 minutes. Serves 6.

This dish is exciting to make, and the recipe is excellent and easy to follow. Do not feel that you must have a paella pan even though they are very much in vogue right now. Search through your cupboards and improvise. Some casseroles and roasters will do. One of the new woks on the market is designed so that its lid is a paella pan. This dish is a show stopper from sunny Spain.

Seafood Quiche

Makes 2 pies

1   package 2 9-inch pie shells,
    or make your own (unbaked)
1½ cups chopped shrimp, cooked, shelled and deveined
6   ounces crab meat (frozen may be used, thaw first)
8   ounces natural Swiss cheese, chopped
½   cup finely chopped celery
½   cup finely chopped scallions
1   cup mayonnaise
2   tablespoons flour
1   cup dry white wine
4   beaten eggs

Combine crab, shrimp, cheese, celery and scallions. Divide mixture into the 2 pie shells. Mix remaining ingredients. Divide and pour evenly over the mixture in the 2 pie shells. Bake at 350° for 35 to 40 minutes.

New England Clam Chowder

This is soooo easy, using the canned clams.

3   6-ounce cans minced clams or fresh clams
6   slices bacon, fried and crumbled
1   medium onion, finely diced
2   stalks celery, finely diced
3   medium potatoes, boiled and cut into small cubes
¼   cup flour
2   tablespoons butter
3½ cups milk, plus juice from the clams

Gently fry onion and celery in small amount of oil until transparent, set aside. Melt butter and add flour, stir until smooth. Add milk and clam juice, stir until slightly thickened. Add the reserved celery and onion, the potatoes, clams, bacon and salt, to taste. Do not boil. Makes 4 to 6 servings.

White Clam Sauce for Pasta

- ¼ cup olive oil
- 1 clove garlic, thinly sliced or crushed
- ¼ cup white wine
- ½ teaspoon chopped parsley
- ½ teaspoon salt
- ¼ teaspoon oregano
- ½ teaspoon black pepper
- 1 cup (8-ounce can) whole or chopped clams in juice

Heat garlic with oil in skillet until lightly browned. Slowly stir in wine. Stir in seasonings; add clams. Cook slowly 15 to 20 minutes until clams are heated thoroughly. Serve over cooked spaghetti.

For variety, prepare sauce as above and then boil your rice in the mixture. It makes a different dish altogether.

This sauce freezes beautifully, so triple the recipe for your family

Red Clam Sauce:

Follow above directions for White Clam Sauce, but add a large can of crushed tomatoes (1 pound 14 ounces) and simmer for at least a half hour.

Maryland Seafood Stew

    3   *large onions, chopped*
   1/2   *cup olive or vegetable oil*
    1   *quart water*
    2   *cups dry red or white wine*
    2   *10-ounce cans tomato paste*
    1   *tablespoon sugar*
    1   *tablespoon salt*
    1   *teaspoon oregano*
    1   *teaspoon basil*
    1   *teaspoon pepper*
   2/3   *cup parsley flakes*
    1   *pound skinless fish fillets*
    1   *pound crabmeat*
    3   *dozen combined soft shell clams, cherrystone clams
         and/or oysters, in shell*

In a large pan, saute onions in oil until tender. Add water, wine, tomato puree and seasonings. Simmer, covered, 1 hour. Wash fish fillets and cut into 6 pieces. Remove cartilage from crabmeat. Scrub clam and/or oyster shells well with a brush. Add the shellfish to the broth first and cook for 20 to 30 minutes, or until the shells open. Then add the fish and/or scallops and cook another 6 to 10 minutes. Makes 6 servings. Crab claws which are very colorful and tasty may also be used.

Boiled Whole Lobster

People have devised many methods of cooking whole lobsters, but the easiest, and most popular, is the boiling method.

Select active live lobsters. Allow a 1 to 1½ pound lobster for each serving. Fill a large pot with enough water to cover the lobsters. Add salt and bring to a rapid boil. (Use 2 tablespoons of salt to each quart of water.)

Plunge the lobster, headfirst into the rapidly boiling, salted water. Bring back to a boil; then reduce heat and simmer:

15 minutes — 1 pound lobsters
20 minutes — 1½ to 2 pound lobsters
40 minutes — very large lobsters

Remove from hot water.

Place on rack. With sharp knife, cut in half lengthwise. Discard all organs in body section near head except red coral roe (in females only) and brownish green liver. Remove black vein that runs to tip of tail. Crack claws. Serve with melted butter.

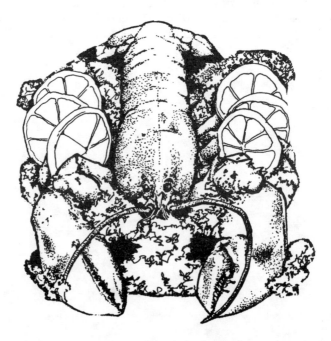